this journal belongs to:

_____

365 days of gratitude
52 weeks of celebration
12 months of mindfulness

WRITE YOUR FAVORITE QUOTE,
POEM OR MANTRA BELOW.

WHAT WAS THE BEST PART OF YOUR DAY?
• write at least one thing every day •

DATE

DATE

DATE

DATE

DATE

DATE

DATE

breathe

WEEK 2

WHAT WAS THE BEST PART OF YOUR DAY?
• write at least one thing every day •

DATE

DATE

DATE

DATE

DATE

DATE

DATE

BREATHE. LEARN. LET GO.

NEVER BE AFRAID TO MAKE YOUR OWN WAVES

SOME THINGS THAT I WANT TO DO MORE OFTEN

- ▲
- ▲
- ▲
- ▲
- ▲
- ▲
- ▲

WHAT WAS THE BEST PART OF YOUR DAY?
• write at least one thing every day •

DATE

DATE

DATE

DATE

DATE

DATE

DATE

WEEK 3

MY ARMS ARE REACHING OUT LIKE SUNRISE.
IT'S A NEW DAY WITH A SKY FULL OF PROMISE.

A SLOW ASCEND.

AND NOW I REMEMBER WHY
NOTHING BEAUTIFUL HAPPENS QUICKLY.

GROWING ALWAYS TAKES TIME—
LIKE SEASONS.
LIKE CHANGE.

WEEK
4

WHAT WAS THE BEST PART OF YOUR DAY?
• write at least one thing every day •

DATE

DATE

DATE

DATE

DATE

DATE

DATE

THINGS THAT TAKE TIME
· ADD TO THE LIST ·

HEALING, GROWING, BECOMING,

WEEK 5

WHAT WAS THE BEST PART OF YOUR DAY?
• write at least one thing every day •

DATE

DATE

DATE

DATE

DATE

DATE

DATE

YOU ARE ALWAYS
ENOUGH LIGHT

.
.
.

WEEK 6

WHAT WAS THE BEST PART OF YOUR DAY?

• write at least one thing every day •

DATE

DATE

DATE

DATE

DATE

DATE

DATE

I AM NOT
WHERE YOU
LEFT ME,
I AM ALL
THE PLACES
I HAVE NEVER
BEEN.

WEEK 7

WHAT WAS THE BEST PART OF YOUR DAY?
• write at least one thing every day •

DATE

DATE

DATE

DATE

DATE

DATE

DATE

PLACES I HAVE BEEN	PLACES I WANT TO GO

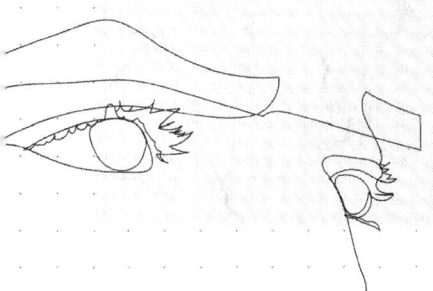

WEEK 8

WHAT WAS THE BEST PART OF YOUR DAY?
• write at least one thing every day •

DATE

DATE

DATE

DATE

DATE

DATE

DATE

COLLECT
MOMENTS, MEMORIES
AND WISHES
. . .
WRITE THEM ON THIS PAGE

WEEK 9

WHAT WAS THE BEST PART OF YOUR DAY?
• write at least one thing every day •

DATE

DATE

DATE

DATE

DATE

DATE

DATE

WEEK 10

WRITE DOWN SOMETHING GOOD.

WRITE DOWN SOMETHING TRUE.

WRITE DOWN SOMETHING BEAUTIFUL.

WHAT WAS THE BEST PART OF YOUR DAY?
• write at least one thing every day •

DATE

DATE

DATE

DATE

DATE

DATE

DATE

WHAT WAS THE BEST PART OF YOUR DAY?
• write at least one thing every day •

DATE

DATE

DATE

DATE

DATE

DATE

DATE

I HAVE WEPT FOR BEAUTIFUL THINGS
RAISING FLOWERS WITH MY RAIN

WEEK 12

WHEN WAS THE LAST TIME SOMETHING BROUGHT YOU TO (HAPPY) TEARS? WHAT DO YOU REMEMBER MOST ABOUT THAT MOMENT?

WRITE ABOUT IT HERE:

WHAT WAS THE BEST PART OF YOUR DAY?
• write at least one thing every day •

DATE

DATE

DATE

DATE

DATE

DATE

DATE

THIS IS YOUR PLACE TO REST. LET GO OF YOUR THOUGHTS AND RELEASE THE THINGS YOU CANNOT CONTROL. SET THEM FREE HERE:

WEEK 13

WHAT WAS THE BEST PART OF YOUR DAY?
• write at least one thing every day •

DATE

DATE

DATE

DATE

DATE

DATE

DATE

WEEK 14

REACH. KEEP REACHING.
BECAUSE THE THINGS WORTH HOLDING
ARE NEVER HANDED TO YOU.

A FEW THINGS THAT I WANT TO
WORK TOWARDS IN THE NEAR FUTURE:

-

-

-

WHAT WAS THE BEST PART OF YOUR DAY?
• write at least one thing every day •

DATE

DATE

DATE

DATE

DATE

DATE

DATE

WEEK 15

IT ISN'T
ALWAYS
GRACEFUL,
BUT BECOMING
NEVER IS.

WHAT WAS THE BEST PART OF YOUR DAY?
• write at least one thing every day •

DATE

DATE

DATE

DATE

DATE

DATE

DATE

WHAT BEAUTIFUL THINGS DO YOU NOTICE WHILE LOOKING OUT OF AN OPEN WINDOW?

(WRITE IN THE SPACE BELOW.)

WEEK 16

WHAT WAS THE BEST PART OF YOUR DAY?
• write at least one thing every day •

DATE

DATE

DATE

DATE

DATE

DATE

DATE

LETTING GO IS HARD,
BUT BEING FREE IS BEAUTIFUL.

WEEK 17

WHAT WAS THE BEST PART OF YOUR DAY?
• write at least one thing every day •

DATE

DATE

DATE

DATE

DATE

DATE

DATE

WEEK 18

THINK ABOUT THE GREATEST
ADVENTURE OF YOUR LIFE (SO FAR),
FILL THIS PAGE WITH WORDS THAT DESCRIBE THAT MOMENT

WHAT WAS THE BEST PART OF YOUR DAY?
• write at least one thing every day •

DATE

DATE

DATE

DATE

DATE

DATE

DATE

WEEK 19

SOMETIMES
ALL THAT MATTERS
IS THAT YOU'RE STILL
TRYING

WHAT WAS THE BEST PART OF YOUR DAY?
• write at least one thing every day •

DATE

DATE

DATE

DATE

DATE

DATE

DATE

DEAR SELF,

WEEK 20

WHAT WAS THE BEST PART OF YOUR DAY?
• write at least one thing every day •

DATE

DATE

DATE

DATE

DATE

DATE

DATE

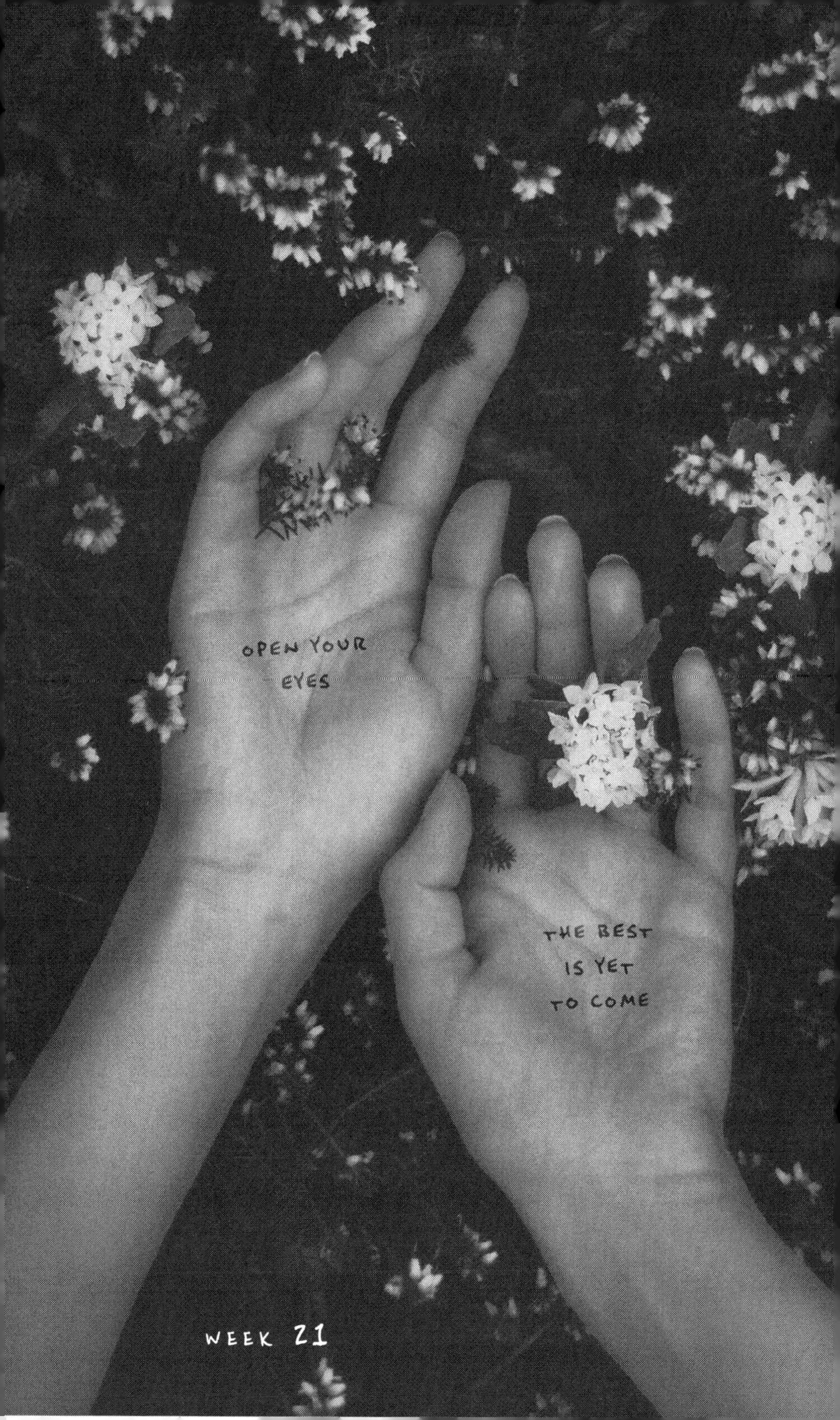
OPEN YOUR
EYES
THE BEST
IS YET
TO COME
WEEK 21

WHAT WAS THE BEST PART OF YOUR DAY?
• write at least one thing every day •

DATE

DATE

DATE

DATE

DATE

DATE

DATE

A LIST OF SIMPLE THINGS THAT MAKE ME HAPPY

_____

_____

_____

_____

_____

_____

_____

_____

_____

_____

WEEK 22

WE ALL FALL
BEFORE WE FEEL
OUR ABILITY
TO FLY

WHAT WAS THE BEST PART OF YOUR DAY?
• write at least one thing every day •

DATE

DATE

DATE

DATE

DATE

DATE

DATE

DON'T LOOK
TO THE GROUND
BECAUSE YOUR SHADOW
STANDS TALL.
YOUR EYES ARE MEANT
TO KNOW THE LIGHT.

WEEK 23

WHAT WAS THE BEST PART OF YOUR DAY?
• write at least one thing every day •

DATE

DATE

DATE

DATE

DATE

DATE

DATE

WEEK 24

WHAT WAS THE BEST PART OF YOUR DAY?
• write at least one thing every day •

DATE

DATE

DATE

DATE

DATE

DATE

DATE

WEEK 25

MY FAVORITE PART
ABOUT THE CURRENT SEASON IS:

WHAT WAS THE BEST PART OF YOUR DAY?
• write at least one thing every day •

DATE

DATE

DATE

DATE

DATE

DATE

DATE

A FEW THINGS THAT I AM GRATEFUL FOR IN THIS MOMENT
(FILL THE EMPTY SPACE BELOW)

WEEK 26

WHAT WAS THE BEST PART OF YOUR DAY?

• write at least one thing every day •

DATE

DATE

DATE

DATE

DATE

DATE

DATE

SHE NEVER WANTED
TO BELONG,
SHE WANTED TO
BE FREE.

WEEK 27

WHAT WAS THE BEST PART OF YOUR DAY?
• write at least one thing every day •

DATE

DATE

DATE

DATE

DATE

DATE

DATE

WEEK 28

I FEEL MOST ALIVE WHEN I

WHAT WAS THE BEST PART OF YOUR DAY?
• write at least one thing every day •

DATE

DATE

DATE

DATE

DATE

DATE

DATE

WEEK 29

A PERFECT DAY BEGINS WITH
_____

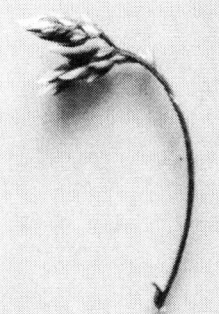

A PERFECT DAY ENDS WITH
_____

WHAT WAS THE BEST PART OF YOUR DAY?
• write at least one thing every day •

DATE

DATE

DATE

DATE

DATE

DATE

DATE

THAT'S THE THING
ABOUT BEING ONE WITH THE WILD,
YOU'RE ALWAYS GROWING.

WEEK 30

WHAT WAS THE BEST PART OF YOUR DAY?
• write at least one thing every day •

DATE

DATE

DATE

DATE

DATE

DATE

DATE

I BELIEVE IN LIVING A LIFE THAT...

WEEK 31

WHAT WAS THE BEST PART OF YOUR DAY?
• write at least one thing every day •

DATE

DATE

DATE

DATE

DATE

DATE

DATE

As the sun rises
the dawn of a new day
I will spread my wings
and go my own way

WEEK 32

WHAT WAS THE BEST PART OF YOUR DAY?
• write at least one thing every day •

DATE

DATE

DATE

DATE

DATE

DATE

DATE

What will bring you home, back to the light?
Share your thoughts

week 33

WHAT WAS THE BEST PART OF YOUR DAY?
• write at least one thing every day •

DATE

DATE

DATE

DATE

DATE

DATE

DATE

WEEK 34

WHAT WAS THE BEST PART OF YOUR DAY?
• write at least one thing every day •

DATE

DATE

DATE

DATE

DATE

DATE

DATE

Fall in love with the thoughts
flowing through your mind
and a willingness to be kind
Fall in love with the open sky
and the tallest tree.
Fall in love with opening your soul
and embracing whatever will be

week 35

WHAT WAS THE BEST PART OF YOUR DAY?
• write at least one thing every day •

DATE

DATE

DATE

DATE

DATE

DATE

DATE

WEEK 36

YOU ARE A TINY SPARK OF JOY,

YOUR LIGHT MAKES A DIFFERENCE IN THIS WORLD.

IF YOU COULD CHANGE THE WORLD

WHAT WOULD YOU DO?

WHAT WAS THE BEST PART OF YOUR DAY?
• write at least one thing every day •

DATE

DATE

DATE

DATE

DATE

DATE

DATE

RUN WILD, RUN FREE,
BE EVERYTHING YOU KNOW YOU CAN BE

WEEK 37

WHAT WAS THE BEST PART OF YOUR DAY?
• write at least one thing every day •

DATE

DATE

DATE

DATE

DATE

DATE

DATE

HEALING ALWAYS TAKES TIME

WEEK 38

WHAT WAS THE BEST PART OF YOUR DAY?
• write at least one thing every day •

DATE

DATE

DATE

DATE

DATE

DATE

DATE

WEEK 39

WHAT WAS THE BEST PART OF YOUR DAY?
• write at least one thing every day •

DATE

DATE

DATE

DATE

DATE

DATE

DATE

THIS IS A BLANK SLATE
(WRITE ABOUT THE THINGS YOU WANT TO ACHIEVE)

WEEK 40

WHAT WAS THE BEST PART OF YOUR DAY?
• write at least one thing every day •

DATE

DATE

DATE

DATE

DATE

DATE

DATE

WEEK 41

EVERY PHASE OF LIGHT TEACHES YOU
TO GROW AND TO HEAL
YOU ARE VALID IN ALL THE THINGS
YOU FEEL

WHAT WAS THE BEST PART OF YOUR DAY?
• write at least one thing every day •

DATE

DATE

DATE

DATE

DATE

DATE

DATE

WHAT SONG MEANS THE MOST TO YOU?
WRITE YOUR FAVORITE LYRICS BELOW...

WEEK 42

WHAT WAS THE BEST PART OF YOUR DAY?
• write at least one thing every day •

DATE

DATE

DATE

DATE

DATE

DATE

DATE

WEEK 43

WHAT IS YOUR MOST CHERISHED MEMORY OF A FRIEND?

HOW DO YOU WANT TO BE REMEMBERED?

WHAT WAS THE BEST PART OF YOUR DAY?
• write at least one thing every day •

DATE

DATE

DATE

DATE

DATE

DATE

DATE

WRITE A LIST OF THINGS THAT YOU ARE PASSIONATE ABOUT.

WEEK 44

WHAT WAS THE BEST PART OF YOUR DAY?
• write at least one thing every day •

DATE

DATE

DATE

DATE

DATE

DATE

DATE

WEEK 45

You are the greatest friend
you will have
Show strength in your battles,
forgive your mistakes
Be kind to yourself
when your heart aches

WHAT WAS THE BEST PART OF YOUR DAY?
• write at least one thing every day •

DATE

DATE

DATE

DATE

DATE

DATE

DATE

WEEK 46

A JOURNEY IS NOT MEASURED IN TIME OR LENGTH,
BUT RATHER EACH SIGNIFICANT STEP
WHAT JOURNEY ARE YOU ON? WRITE ABOUT IT!

WHAT WAS THE BEST PART OF YOUR DAY?
• write at least one thing every day •

DATE

DATE

DATE

DATE

DATE

DATE

DATE

WEEK 47

WHAT WAS THE BEST PART OF YOUR DAY?
• write at least one thing every day •

DATE

DATE

DATE

DATE

DATE

DATE

DATE

WHAT IS HAPPENING TODAY THAT YOU WISH TO CHANGE TOMORROW?

WEEK 48

WHAT WAS THE BEST PART OF YOUR DAY?
• write at least one thing every day •

DATE

DATE

DATE

DATE

DATE

DATE

DATE

WHAT DOES SELF DISCOVERY MEAN TO YOU?
LIST THE THINGS YOU HAVE
DISCOVERED ABOUT YOURSELF RECENTLY.

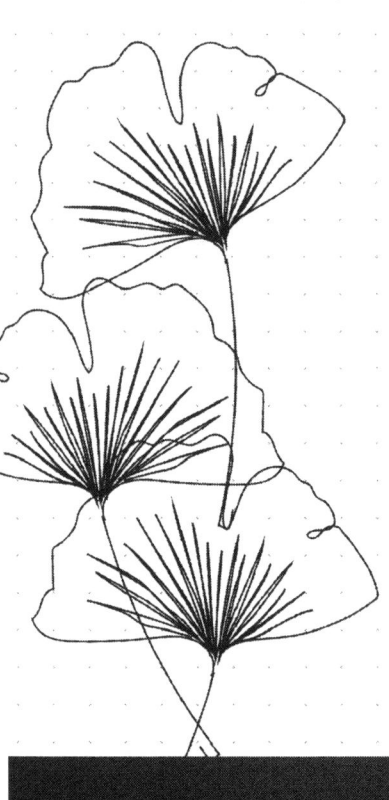

WEEK 49

WHAT WAS THE BEST PART OF YOUR DAY?
• write at least one thing every day •

DATE

DATE

DATE

DATE

DATE

DATE

DATE

WEEK 50

FLOWERS GROW TOWARDS THE SUN

ALWAYS CHASING THE LIGHT

AND SO SHOULD YOU

SURROUND YOURSELF WITH THE

THINGS THAT HELP YOU GROW

SEIZE EVERY NEW DAY

BIG, BOLD AND BRIGHT

WHAT WAS THE BEST PART OF YOUR DAY?
• write at least one thing every day •

DATE

DATE

DATE

DATE

DATE

DATE

DATE

HOW HAVE YOU GROWN?

WEEK 51

WHAT WAS THE BEST PART OF YOUR DAY?
• write at least one thing every day •

DATE

DATE

DATE

DATE

DATE

DATE

DATE

WHAT HOPE WILL TOMORROW BRING?
LIST THE THINGS THAT WILL MAKE IT EASIER BELOW

WEEK 52

WHAT WAS THE BEST PART OF YOUR DAY?
• write at least one thing every day •

DATE

DATE

DATE

DATE

DATE

DATE

DATE

Made in the USA
San Bernardino, CA
12 December 2019